CW00658811

fatal WOMEN

Kevin Nicholas Roberts

Published by CC Productions
Paradise Farm
Westhall, Halesworth
Suffolk IP19 8RH

Also by Kevin Nicholas Roberts

Quest for the Beloved

Published by CC Productions
Paradise Farm
Westhall, Halesworth
Suffolk IP19 8RH

© 2000 CC Productions

Kevin Nicholas Roberts is hereby identified as the author
of this work in accordance with Section 77 of the
Copyright, Designs and Patents Act 1988.

All rights reserved. No part of this publication may be
reproduced in any form or by any means, without prior
written permission from the author.

Front Cover: Ophelia, 1910, by John William Waterhouse
Private Collection/Julian Hartnoll/Bridgeman Art Library

ISBN 1 85525 047 0

Design by Red Hot Media, Lowestoft

Printed & Bound by Richardson Printing, Lowestoft

To my dear friend Carmen,
and to Algernon Charles Swinburne,

these poems
are affectionately and admiringly
dedicated.

Introduction

The archetype of the femme fatale has existed and persisted in fascinating writers from time immemorial. She appears in the mythology of nearly every known culture, taking such seductive forms as siren and mermaid, witch and succubus, courtesan and vampire, moon goddess and fairy queen. She has been the focal point of countless poets and playwrights, including such masters as John Milton, Edgar Allan Poe and William Shakespeare. And, perhaps most intriguingly, she is a central figure in the religious texts of both Eastern and Western traditions. Within this context, she has been called Kali, Mary Magdelene, Dalila, Salome and, of course, Eve, the mother of all fatal women. However, this eternal seductress seems to have been of particular interest to the Neoclassical and Victorian Romantic poets, each of whom lent to her his own singular passion and unique psychology.

As the vast majority of celebrated poets during these literary periods were young males, the female naturally assumed the role of Other. Her nature and her motivations were unknown, mysterious and consequently perceived as dangerous. Woman possessed an arcane power that was frightening because it could be neither understood nor controlled by the male. Her power was a kind of natural force whose potency issued from the deepest spaces of Man's unconscious, affecting him at a primal level. Thus, the femme fatale in Romantic poetry became associated with the macabre. She was, in essence, a disturbing reflection of the intense ambivalence toward women and love harboured by the young men writing about her.

For John Keats, La Belle Dame sans Merci is a beautiful, bewitching lady who "lulled" the poet, the knight-at-arms, "pale kings and princes too" into their graves with her irresistible "fairy song." To fall in love (or lust) with her is to invite a broken heart, at least, and ultimately madness and death. In this sense, she is the personification of 'wasting love,' the kind of love that seduces the poet into relinquishing his soul, the kind of love that makes nothing else matter. She is wild in a way that makes men hungry to possess her, while knowing all along that she will not be possessed. In short, she is a trap in which some part of the poet desires to be caught, despite (and, in some cases, because of) the deadly consequences.

La Belle Dame sans Merci, or the beautiful woman without mercy, is also beguiling because she represents what Samuel Taylor Coleridge referred to as a "reconciliation of opposites." That is, she embodies the qualities of the innocent as well as the corrupt, the ideal in combination with the defiled. In this way, she is a kind of monster, simultaneously beautiful and grotesque, irresistible and repulsive, sacred and profane. She is both angel and devil, virgin and whore. Most importantly, she is never what she appears to be. She may be our redeemer or the source of our damnation. She is equally nocturnal and diurnal. She is non-human, a fairy-woman, both more and less than Man. And, on some level, it is that inhumanness that makes her so erotic.

In *Fatal Women*, Kevin Roberts has recreated this seductive figure in an intriguing variety of sumptuous images. There is Allayne. Demon and Saint. Seducer and Destroyer. As an archetype of danger, she provokes the blackest desires, and for those lured by her favours, payment is severe. Mortiche, on the other hand, is the expression of the idealised lover, all consuming in her innocence and worshiped with tenderness by the poet. And Clayre? Clayre is ambiguous, evasive, also the most subtle in fulfilment. She is the eternal Eve -the icon of the Feminine- shifting between earth, heaven and hell, never quite known, never entirely possessed. She is unveiled with extreme caution.

In these hauntingly sensuous poems, the fatal woman is still a romantic paradox, both enticing and terrifying; however, for Roberts her allure goes beyond the physical and psychological to include a kind of erotic spirituality. For him, the femme fatale is also the divine Beloved, the soul mate, the ideal feminine with which the poet aspires to reconnect. She is attainable, though temporarily out of his reach. She may protest; she may even destroy the poet (or herself), but she can never escape him for long.

Contents

The darker side of our love,
A lighter shade of death.
That thing that brings me comfort:
The sweet sleeping sound of your breath.

K.N.R.

Christine

No longer light, but not yet dark,
We stand here in some space between
And listen to a meadow lark;
Last year she sang so sweet and keen
For us, Christine.

Here amid the fading flowers,
We think of things that shall not be.
Christine, can you recall the hours
When I was you and you were me
Beside the sea?

Above our heads, the soul of day
Moves softly through the autumn skies;
The earth gives up its green to grey,
And there before our stinging eyes,
It stirs and dies.

The crow plays in the golden grass
And grieves not at his final flight;
He knows that all good things must pass,
That darkness always follows light.
It seems he's right.

Christine, you fall away from me
On this dour late autumn day
As fiery leaves forsake the tree,
Like eager seeds that drift away
In search of May.

Your fervent mouth looks different now,
The tongue less sweet, the lips less keen,
But press its heat against my brow....
Those lips, I think, have never been
So cold, Christine.

And now that autumn chills our breath,
The light that lit your loving eyes
Fades fast towards a silent death,
And dies now as the season dies,
With subtle sighs.

Go not as one whose steps would sever;
Christine, no shred of sorrow show.
As if farewell were not for-ever,
Go forth like snowflakes, soft and slow,
Like lovers go.

Withhold the tears that you would weep,
And with a smile avert your face,
As though you've turned aside to sleep
And soon will wake to claim your place
In my embrace.

Your leaving shall not be the last;
Where e'er you look, there I will be.
And like fond phantoms from the past,
The wild winds that sweep the sea
Bring you to me.

And spectres of our summer showers
Shall dance on in my memory,
The promises of perfect hours,
When I was you and you were me,
Beside the sea.

Rondel

Our time has passed on swift and careless feet,
With sighs and smiles and songs both sad and sweet.
Our perfect hours have grown and gone so fast,
And these are things we never can repeat.
Though we might plead and pray that it would last,
Our time has passed.

Like shreds of mist entangled in a tree,
Like surf and sea-foam on a foaming sea,
Like all good things we know can never last,
Too soon we'll see the end of you and me.
Despite the days and dreams that we amassed,
Our time has passed.

Carmen

In dreams of her – a wild dim world of dreams,
Like waking sleep, these distant days with her – it seems
A wild dim world and she a wan wildflower
Abloom, abud, ablaze in an amourous hour:
A flower that neither God nor frenzied wind would stir...
In dreams of her.

Tonight, I heard the wingéd faery sighs
For Carmen's lips and for her bright brown eyes,
And even God did sigh and in his gilded sleep did stir
With dreams of her.

Mortiche

As the evening light repines about me
And the willow weeps against the glass,
Soft my lover sleeps in bliss beside me,
Soft the hours, pensive, pass,
Mortiche, alas!

Amongst the cushions where you sleep,
Reclining, lost to distant dreams,
So far away you are, and deep;
And though my mouth would smile, it seems,
Mortiche, I weep.

You would not think it possible for Man to tease
The outline of his darkest need, I know, and yet,
I have, and still cannot appease
My soul, his aching sin; I was beset
When first we met.

But now the silent weeks have flown,
The hours fled.
And all the dreams we dared to own
In our shared bed—
They have been said.

And here, to me, you lie so close
All honey-spice and jessamine;
I can touch you in your dark repose
And know sweet breath upon my skin.
And still, Mortiche, you seem a sin.

So long I yearned to kiss your eyes;
In dreams their deepest depths I'd plumb
And drown beneath your pleasur'd sighs
Like lovers bathed in opium.
I fear'd the hour would never come.

But it was always this day.
And it was ever this hour.
And every soul, it seems, must Time obey,
Even you within your ghosted tower,
As every May forfeits its flower.

And now I watch you while you sleep,
Unknowing, as I dimly trace
The tears of helplessness I weep
In outline o'er your classic face,
With tender grace.

For now, my love, our path is set.
Submit I must, and bow to Fate,
And smile, and laugh, and thus forget,
And pray you not to wake too late.
Mortiche, I wait.

It Is Too Late

It is too late. Though we would reinspire
Our dream, rewake a dead desire,
A dismal sea divides our sighs and smiles;
Between us now, so many months and miles
And tears for all things torn away by time,
For faded flowers grown pale and past their prime.
And no sweet word can make sick joys survive,
No mystic kiss keep loves long dead alive.
What mortal hand can stay the hand of fate?
It is too late.

Clayre

Shades that deck the dusky sky,
That changes hue
With every breeze that billows by,
Change less than you.
Its colours ever-changing;
Its tides so vastly ranging,
And still they change far less than Clayre should do.

It's me alone she loves by night,
But then by day,
When lovers lure her supple sight,
She's borne away.
Her straying glance can gash apart
The chambers of my steady heart;
So, my inconstant Clayre, what would you say?

Your eyes, no doubt, possess with grace
Their fickle stare,
Give magic to your maiden face,
Twice-over fair.
And still a lesser man might trade
Such beauty for a love that stayed,
For all the silken strands of all your hair.

But I, my Love, see only you
And could not cease
To love those eyes that thrill my soul,
Yet yield no peace.
Their fever, like the blushing flowers
Left swaying in the sun for hours,
Gives rise to streams of sighs that still increase.

Your way, I know, no prayer nor plea
Could take away;
No more could I deny the sea
Its surge and sway.
As long as your mood ever ranges
To a love, as one love never changes;
Just as long as no thing ever changes
Your love for me.

Alone

Before you were here, I knew you.
You haunted me, a persistent Spirit, even in my boyhood.
Solitary stones on lonely ponds I played,
Whose every ripple whispered your name.
And in those same still waters, I saw your face,
And I knew that too.
Those eyes, more clear and calm
Than streams or stars or even my youth.
And in the rain, especially lightning summer storms,
Your laughter trickled through the gutters
Of my father's house
And splashed and leapt in tiny puddles,
Black beneath my dim-lit room–
In shining pools of mingled tears.
I wept silently, even then, for you.
Sometimes I thought I heard your voice,
That faery song of my every life,
Sighing through the longing wind-swept nights.
You seemed to me then an impossible dream;
Like sacred music carried on a funereal breeze,
I felt you, singing madly through the night-stained trees.
And whenever I have lain, unassailed,
Beneath the full and wide-eyed Moon,
I have known you there as well.
And by Her light I have wept to know
That you shine on me
Alone.

Ophelia

To be, or not to be, that is the question;
Whether 'tis nobler in the mind to suffer
The slings and arrows of outrageous fortune,
Or to take arms against a sea of troubles,
And by opposing, end them. To die; to sleep,
No more, and by a sleep to say we end
The heart-ache, and the thousand natural shocks
That flesh is heir to; 'tis a consummation
Devoutly to be wish'd, to die, to sleep;
To sleep; perchance to dream...

From Shakespeare's *Hamlet*

Adorned in gold and brilliant blue,
She wandered cheerless in the glade,
Whilst wild about her breezes blew
And yielding boughs about her swayed.
In fragile hands she clasped a flower,
Worn petals of a wasted hour;
She'd touched Love's fragrant fertile bower
And felt its fickle blossom fade.

She prayed her sorrow soon would pass,
That pain would fade with spiteful day,
Like supple serpents in the grass
That graze the foot, then glide away.
She grieved for lies left unaddressed
And secret sins gone unconfessed
And loving words yet unprofessed
By lovers with sad words to say.

She wondered that the world could sever
Mirth from such a man as he,
But knew her love was lost forever,
That what was naught would never be.
She pined for her disparaged prince,
Whose eyes in hers had found offense,
And mourned her martyred innocence
That went the way of destiny.

Who knows what seeds are best to sew
To keep men near and heaven nigh?
But blossoms born and fed by snow
Are soon to freeze and swift to die.
She knew that all the seeds she'd sewn,
That all the girlish dreams she'd known,
Had spread their wearied wings and flown
And reason was the next to fly.

In curling hair that flashed like fire
Tender dreams went down to day.
The dust of wan and wild desire--
Dry brittle bones Time bore away.
So like a dead man's blood and breath,
So everything that perisheth,
Must blossom, bloom, then bleed to death,
And dreams soon fall to dim decay.

She danced with phantoms in the mist
Amid the frailly failing light
And sang of lover's lips that kissed
And stung her like a serpent's bite.
Soft eyes and eyelids swelled with tears
And brimmed with love and foamed with fears
And yearned for used up youthful years
Of easy dreams and meek delight.

She sang of sweeter, softer times
When life was new and love was young
In jangled notes and tangled rhymes
That tore the throat and smote the tongue.
Bright madness stung her burning eyes,
Like churning clouds in sightless skies,
As from her lips a stream of sighs
Sang for a life and love unsung.

And then her strange unseemly smile
Dissolved into a savage scream
That rendered her fair visage vile
And gave red eyes a rabid gleam.
The stars above her blurred and bled
And all her colours ran to red
As through the fields Ophelia fled
And stopped beside a twilit stream.

Her fierce and frantic fingers wound
And wept, for every word he said,
And tore glad grasses from the ground
And wove a garland for her head.
The blowing of her hair unbound,
Her gilded skirts that billowed 'round,
Composed an eerie rustling sound
Like choirs of wretched restless dead.

Lithe limbs and slender shoulders shook,
As raking fingers rent the sedge;
She forged a bed beside the brook
And laughing mouthed a mindless pledge--
And all the while left unaware
That Death heard every whispered prayer
And always knew he'd find her there
That night beside the water's edge.

The sun had set beyond the hill
But left a trace of dusky light;
She noticed not the growing chill,
Acknowledged not the coming night.
She pressed the wreath against her face
And writhed in passion-scented grace
Amidst her dark enchanted place
Of scarlet, black and lily white.

And then appeared before the maiden
Visions of a savage face,
With secret sin and sorrow laden
Bereft of all its former grace;
She shrank beneath the ghosted stare
Of one who once had found her fair
Then clawed the flowers from her hair
And ripped her gown to rags of lace.

She took a last long sobbing breath,
But found she could no longer weep;
Her eager tongue had tasted death
And found it good and drank it deep.
She sought to leave all pain behind
(Her bitter burning love and blind,
That bent and broke her girlish mind)
Within the arms of gentle Sleep.

She slipped inside her watery grot
And sank to where all trouble seems
So far away and soon forgot
Like fading forms in distant dreams.
Her aching spirit swiftly fled
And on her flesh the fishes fed
And drank the warm sweet blood she bled,
Our sleeping lady of the streams.

On Parting

You seem a sad forgotten flower
Plucked from some placid fairy-place,
Flushed and flecked with fear, your dreaming-flower's
face,
Damp with dew and dread;
A savage bleeding bloom, your hue
A streaming eye and swollen eyelid red.

That I might stay another blessed hour
To kiss the tears from parted petal-lips,
Take further refuge in your fairy power
Another day, one last good night,
And hold a hand more bright and sweet, now lost,
Than even love is sweet and bright.

Allayne

The dawn of day is drawing near—
Would that explain
Why I should wake and find you here,
My lost Allayne?

I see you wear the look of saints,
The face you feign,
To hide the hungry beast that waits
To strike, Allayne.

But parted lips betray the thirst
You can't restrain,
And kissing them would make them burst
And bleed, Allayne.

So relish now the single kiss
Real love has lain,
And when you die, remember this
In hell, Allayne:

To love you was my single sin—
Could I abstain?
Fair flesh has felled far better men
Than I, Allayne.

Your perfect mouth was made to please
And bring me pain
With brazen teeth that taunt and tease
My soul, Allayne.

That I should chasten you by the rod
The gods ordain.
What breed of fierce infernal god
Forged you, Allayne?

What sort of strange sadistic spawn,
What brand of bane,
Made you a dark delicious pawn
Of death, Allayne?

When you were born, the devil swore
He would obtain
Your body and the soul it bore
With shame, Allayne.

Your Lord's perversely pulsing heart
Was torn in twain
That he might place the blackest part
In you, Allayne.

But when he tore you from the womb
Did you complain,
Or did you like his torrid tomb
Much more, Allayne?

He filled you with each kind of curse
You could contain,
And left you with a lust far worse
Than his, Allayne.

Henceforth you were his cherished prize
And chatelaine;
You rule his world of grim demise
With glee, Allayne.

You hold his horde of fiends in thrall,
A queen you reign,
And walk in shadows where they fall,
By night, Allayne.

And though you hate me for it, yet
I still maintain,
I love you, though you would forget
I lived, Allayne.

A sweet and subtly scented sea,
Your splendid mane
Excites my soul, enticing me
To drown, Allayne.

Your shameless cryptic shoulder's curve
Is half profane;
It shifts with fire in every nerve
That burns, Allayne.

But of your charms that mesmerise
And seek to chain,
Your brilliant black voracious eyes
Are best, Allayne.

They seethe with all the eager slaves
Your love has slain;
You sent them gladly to their graves
Alone, Allayne.

The pressure of your piercing teeth
Would prick the vein
And draw the flood that flows beneath
The flesh, Allayne.

The fragments of their fleeting lives
Would rush and rain
To feed the fiendish life that thrives
In you, Allayne.

You flourish by the fevered lips
And life you drain;
With lusty sighs and hungry sips
You drink, Allayne.

You seem a vile envenomed thing
And less than sane;
Your kiss so like a serpent's sting
Can kill, Allayne.

The poison in that brutal kiss
Now wracks my brain
And sends my blood to mortal bliss
In you, Allayne.

Against your scarlet silken dress
The nipples strain
And raise to meet the hard caress
You crave, Allayne.

But you could never stoop to love,
Nor would you deign
To hold a mortal man above
Yourself, Allayne.

Your only longing is for death
And things arcane;
Your breathing is the tainted breath
Of tombs, Allayne.

Destroying me will be the cost,
And what you gain
Is freedom from the soul you lost
Long since, Allayne.

But when I'm gone will you forget,
Or entertain,
The passions you could not permit
To grow, Allayne?

I've one last wish, but would my wishing
Be in vain?
Just once, I'd hear the hateful thing
You hide, Allayne.

So now I ask you to confess,
By love of Cain,
The joy it gives you to possess
My gift, Allayne.

I leave you something that will stay,
A fatal stain,
That you could never wash away
With blood, Allayne.

The touch of my deferring hand
You will retain,
A touch you may well understand
In time, Allayne.

Until the end of all your days
It will remain,
And then the fiend you dared to praise
Will fall, Allayne.

Angelic armies will descend
And him arraign;
They'll bring about his brutal end
On earth, Allayne.

The remnant of his writing form
Will wax and wane
And perish in a reeking storm
Of dust, Allayne.

You'll stand alone to face the fall
Of his domain
And watch the ruin of every wall
He built, Allayne.

And then, my love, we both will see
If you disdain
The only soul that would not flee
Your touch, Allayne.

I sink into the strangest sleep,
Whilst you sustain;
As dark as death and twice as deep
I doze, Allayne.

With death die all my mortal fears
I shan't regain,
And I can wait a swarm of years
For you, Allayne.

You think you've seen the last of me,
Your slavish swain,
But mine will be the face you see
 In dreams, Allayne.

I swear it now, my wicked thing,
We'll meet again.
Then will you wear the devil's ring...
Or mine, Allayne?

Orpheus

Fair phantom notes flow from thy lips
    On breath made sweet with supple sighs;
Thy song, in soft and savage sips,
    The gods would drink with half-closed eyes.
Your music sooth'd the souls of men
    And moved the winds and stir'd the trees -
Forever, now, sweet Orpheus,
    It haunts the seas.

The savage sea, its surge and sway
    Of clutching waves and barren deep
Sang soft thy dirge, then bore away
    Thy sleepless life of lifeless sleep.
The gods who tore thee left a trace
    Of former fairness, for it seems
You feign the voice of one awake, the face
    Of one who dreams.

The glancing blow, the blow that smote,
    Harsh payment for thy single sin,
Unsexed thee by thy severed throat
    And left thee loathe and least of men.
O lustful women! Whores of Fate!
    All envious of Eurydice
They lured her in and locked the gates
  of Paradise.

Hyacinthe

Like splendid seas and faultless as a flower
And aptly called by flushing flower's name,
With sad sweet voice possessed of fairy power
That made me love long ere we met, the same
As had we loved some lost long fevered hour
In frenzied throes, with flesh and lips aflame.

Smooth-skinned and white, with soft pale throat perfumed
And languid limbs that cry to be caressed
And kissed and clutched and full-consumed,
Her passioned lips half-mad to be possessed:
Asleep, alone, with mermaid-dreams entombed,
She waits, frail hands laid light upon her chest.

Mad dreams drone past of maiden pleasures missed,
A flood of fears and subtle, silent sighs,
Half-parted lips, as though they've just been kissed,
Half-haunted eyes grown wide and wild and wise,
Reflecting shades, like ghosted clouds of mist,
But clear and calm like sultry seas and skies.

A kiss to wake forgotten fairy powers!
One hallowed touch to conjure sacred sight!
A heart that bleeds to show what shall be ours
In starry eyes so soft and warm and bright:
A swarm of savage, sad, redemptive stars
In some eternal sacrificial night.

Elfin Charms

Spin your elfin charms,
And from mad fingers
Let glad silks unwinde
Angelic webs
With silver'd souls entwined.

And fly you now into the Night
On current light and whisp'ry warm.
Appear to me in faerie form,
From out of love's undying storm—
To cast your spell, my midnight dream!

How boldly we'll invoke the Moon—
Our passioned tongues of sacred fire!
We'll pray to Her we would inspire
To bend Her will to our desire.

Then I will take your tiny hand
And press it, sweet, among the stones,
Though just beneath our feet
The bones of saints and madmen long forgot
Of warning sigh in spectral tones.

But heed them not, these buried seers;
They only seek to try our fears!
But we have waited countless years,
And even now the hour nears
When love shall kiss away our tears!

Come! Tarry not, my ageless one.
Forget for now this cold dead place,
For the Moon has knelt and brushed your face
And to our goal She lends Her grace--
To be as one in Her embrace.

Listen. There! Upon the mist!
On wind-swept leaves they float along--
Soft spirit sighs and whispers long.
They summon us with faerie song.
'Tis to their race that we belong.

Quick! Close your eyes! Cast off blind sight!
Gods won't be caught by candle-light.
With magic we'll pursue the sprite,
Through kingdoms darker than the Night,
On wings composed for moon-lit flight.

Upon the winds of stormy sleep
We'll slide through waves unto the deep,
Where sirens sing and fishes weep
And mermaids dream their blust'ry dreams.

And there, in dark, beneath the waves,
Where sailors sleep in watery graves,
We'll summon sylphs from coral caves
And dance among these holy knaves.

Then 'round us thrice the nix will twist,
And bind our bodies wrist to wrist,
And spin the spell of Paradise
Entwining us in webs of mist.

Then all the creatures of the sea
Will make a myth of our romance,
For only in the strangest trance
May mortals with the fishes dance.

And though 'tis sweet, this watery place,
Against the dawn we two must race.
For when the Sun dost show His face
The faeries fade without a trace.

Awaken now, my lady fair,
And shake the faeries from your hair,
For even as they take to air
Return we must to mortal space
And from this fishy vision tear.

But alas, my love, forget your fears,
And brush away your Asrai tears
For when the Moon to Neptune nears,
(This happens every thousand years!)
Our land of faeries reappears.

And though 'till then we'll be apart,
If you hold this place inside your heart
And dream of mermen, vows and me,
And all other worlds refuse to see,
Then life to death we will impart,
And ever bound we two shall be.

Astrologia

Based on the painting by Edward Burne Jones

What secrets burn behind the glass;
What spirits climb?
What sorry things and sad things pass;
What things sublime;
What fate, unfolding like a book,
For her from whom one brief glance took
All innocence and hope for all of time?

Behind her eyes, where grief is grown,
Desire dies
With sighs for all the sorrows flown
And joy that flies
And fades the blush upon her cheek,
Her eyes so beautiful and bleak,
Their blue the subtle blue of seas and skies.

Though knowing is a kind of curse
She would contain,
She knows not yet which wound is worse,
Which pain more deep -
The pulse of perfect hours fled
Or endless years that lay ahead
With nothing left to do but wait and weep.

Chainmail Angel

Upon the wing of thine own most favoured dove
I have flown to thee here this night, my love.

Open your eyes in the darkness;
Look upon my sad, pale face,
My mad, pale eyes
Burning the night air into ash
And finding you there,
Where it falls,
Scenting your bedsheets with the musky-warm
fragrance
Of the ashes of those blossoms whose blushing petals
I have caressed
And kissed
And spread
To reveal their perfect aching beauty.

You smile, for you think me to be as I have been,
But, alas, the futile deeds,
The wars of men,
Have spilt my blood,
And the boy who left you with a kiss,
So many days and dreams ago,
That boy will never breathe his life between your lips
again.

But I am with you now, my lady,
For we took a vow;
I swore I would return.
And though my flesh has bled its life,
My soul's dead eyes within your chamber burn.

Tonight, the air about me was a storm of angels,
They stir'd the darkness with invisible wings,
And in my own blind fury,
The fatal blindness of my youth,
I met the sword that proved my own mortality a
truth.

The night was sharp;
It cut so deep.
And even as I fell, I heard your voice:

All is lost! All is lost!

Can you forgive me?
For all my pride, our love has been the cost.

And now, though my armoured form lies far away,
Cold, blood-smeared, and all alone,
Staring blindly at the moon,
And being lapped at by the dogs,
I wear my chainmail still,
For it is welded to my eternal soul.

If you can forgive,
Kneel beside me now
As you have knelt so many times before
To kiss my scars,
The purpled, swollen flesh
Of what would have been my victories.

Put your lips to my side;
Touch the flowing, flowering wound
That not even your magical devotion could heal.
Love me,
One last time.

I know–
You will remember,
Taste my body's passion in the salt of your own tears.
And I swear on all I love that we two shall meet again.

But even now the talons tear,
And wing is born of tender flesh and shoulder blade.
And so, my love, forget me,
For the one you know,
This human form you loved,
From this world, tonight, must forever fade.

Skin & Bones

For Carmen, inspired by her poem "Catacomb Chant"

When lightning strikes, you shall see my face:
Outlined, enshrouded, just beyond my velvet grave,
Just beneath your room of glass and flowers.
See inside me then, as I see you:
The fragile brittleness of bone,
The cold, dead blood frozen in my shrunken veins,
The sockets of my eyes....so empty now,
Gone green to black, and stitched against the sun.
Look at me closely then, you, in your warm bed.
And remember me in my crypt of cruel stone.
Know me for what I am; and know yourself,
For both of us are skin and bone.

When thunder crashes, you shall hear my voice,
The same as it has always been.
But now its power is that of your God–
The God who would not let me in.
In that faraway sound that you have so longed to hear,
Find peace, and know that I am near,
Beside you, waiting and forever biding
Time, 'til your own path should lead you here.
Listen for the owl at night.
Talk to him as he were me.
Hold his voice against your face;
Crush it close against your breast.
Keep it warm and loved and safe,
If not for me, then for yourself,
For you and I are both the same.

And when the rain has finally come,
Pecking at your window lattice,
Soft at first, then with insistence,
Have no doubt; I lay without.
Let each drop be as my tears
That burn with years I shared your bed.
And pull the sheets to hide your head,
And clasp your beads, and pray for light.
But never, Sweet, deny nor dread
The coming of our promised night.

The tears of the dead, bitter as they may be, are sweet;
They glisten on your passing breath
And make your sad heart slip a beat,
Your soul to long for easeful death.
How I so long to keep its coursing pace,
To touch the blood-filled blueness of your breathing
face
That lifts from me my crushing stone,
The chill from this eternal place.
Where worms have fed on frozen flesh,
Warm flesh shall lie with ashen bone.

Alone in the Forest

Do you remember the time we were laughing,
Alone in the forest, the face we were seeking?
To know it was hiding inside ourselves,
To know the only truth, and that is Death.
Our hands outstretched before us, feeling
For something in that gaunt darkness,
The place that it can be found,
Where the treacherous mouths of the angels,
Their eyelids peeled back to reveal nothing,
Profess that Nothing lay beyond.

Yet glance into the distance,
Back through time,
To the city that you came from,
To the place of your birth.
Do you know who I am, my Love?
Would you recognise me
If I wore a different face?
What were you thinking....
That we were escaping?
Know this, my Beloved, there is no escape.

The owl in the forest soars whitely
On a canvas, the blue-black of winter.
High above the night he cries;
He calls out your name,
Whispers my own in your tender frozen ear.
His voice will remind you,
Like the empty black eyes of the angels,
Of the city you came from

And the place of your birth.
When he has flown from us this night,
Then shall we know the truth.

And when you peel back the faces
Of the corpses that lay in our path,
At the crossroads before us,
Will you know them by name?
Will they all seem familiar,
Like you knew them before?
Will they wear our two faces
As the dust is blown aside
And the wind reveals our truth?

And the fevered caresses
In the arms of the angels...
Which one is your lover?
Is he the one who wears my face?
But when you peel back my eyelids
And you gaze into Nothing,
There you will see reflected,
In that perfect mute blackness
The reflection of our soul–
Yours and mine.

And the fever that passes
Would want to possess us,
Would want to unsex us;
That is its will.
Do not try to deny it.

For the demon now making its way through the forest
Wears the mask of an angel,
Holds the shape of a man.

The shivers that wrack me now
Are its touching my body,
Licking the spaces between each of my bones.
If you peel back the eyelids
Of the creature that taunts you,
You will find in its darkness
The soul that you love.

The beast that would tear you,
Like the eyes of the angels,
And my touches that break you–
They fill you equally now.
What you hear in the darkness
Is the truth of your body;
The laborious breathing you hear
Is the sound of my soul.

Let them all dance there,
On the tip of your hot red flesh.
They are the same as my warm lips
Entwined in your hair.
If you peel back the silken strands
You might capture me there.

How Sweet the Night

How sweet the night where Death dwells:
Like a dense forest when the snow is falling.
And we, all unknowing, slip closer, drawn deeper,
Lured by the toll of tempestuous bells.

Loving His warm breath, carried on the frozen air—
Transformed into black crystal snowflakes
That caress and bejewel our hair.
In the crystalline moonlight, it is your face I see,
Dancing and spinning just beyond the deepest drifts,
Writhing in your soul's own consumed ecstasy.

And so with your blessing, I would go to Him now,
Should white Death, on this night, cleave Himself unto me.

Kubla Khan

Part One: Coleridge, 1798

In Xanadu did Kubla Khan
A stately pleasure-dome decree:
Where Alph, the sacred river, ran
Through caverns measureless to man
Down to a sunless sea.
So twice five miles of fertile ground
With walls and towers were girdled round:
And there were gardens bright with sinuous rills,
Where blossomed many an incense-bearing tree;
And here were forests ancient as the hills,
Enfolding sunny spots of greenery.

But oh! that deep romantic chasm which slanted
Down the green hill athwart a cedarn cover!
A savage place! as holy and enchanted
As e'er beneath a waning moon was haunted
By woman wailing for her demon-lover!
And from this chasm, with ceaseless turmoil seething,
As if this earth in fast thick pants were breathing,
A mighty fountain momently was forced:
Amid whose swift half-intermitted burst
Huge fragments vaulted like rebounding hail,
Or chaffy grain beneath the thresher's flail:
And 'mid these dancing rocks at once and ever
It flung up momently the sacred river.
Five miles meandering with a mazy motion
Through wood and dale the sacred river ran,
Then reached the caverns measureless to man,
And sank in tumult to a lifeless ocean:

And 'mid this tumult Kubla heard from far
Ancestral voices prophesying war!
The shadow of the dome of pleasure
Floated midway on the waves;
Where was heard the mingled measure
From the fountain and the caves.
It was a miracle of rare device,
A sunny pleasure-dome with caves of ice!

A damsel with a dulcimer
In a vision once I saw:
It was an Abyssinian maid,
And on her dulcimer she played,
Singing of Mount Abora.
Could I revive within me
Her symphony and song,
To such a deep delight 'twoud win me,
That with music loud and long,
I would build that dome in air,
That sunny dome! Those caves of ice!
And all who heard should see them there,
And all should cry, Beware! Beware!
His flashing eyes, his floating hair!
Weave a circle round him thrice,
And close your eyes with holy dread,
For he on honey-dew hath fed,
And drunk the milk of Paradise.

PART TWO: Roberts, 1998

In nighted visions once I heard
The sweetest song Man ever knew.
And as I drowsed, this hallowed sound
Suffused the air, and all else drowned beneath its strain:
It swelled! It grew!
The rarest thing of all things rare!
Heard once before, known once and lost,
And lost with it, my soul sank too.
But when this seraph sang for me,
My spirit burned with bliss anew;
It was the fair Abyssinian maid,
And on her dulcimer she played
A savage music– terrible and true.
And with her symphony and song–
And with her music loud and long–
This strangest angel stroked the strings
That summoned me to Xanadu.

Oh! how my soul within me soared
To see such splendour atop the sacred mount,
Where still my poet-mystic laid,
Still suckling from her honeyed, holy fount,
As she upon his mortal passions played,
In all his fleshly, purpled lust displayed.
His flashing eyes she soft did close
And smoothed his wild, once-floating hair,
And sighed– While still ancestral voices rose:
Of raging war did they declare.
And wretched, bloodied spectres cried in wailing tones:

"Beware! Beware! The sainted Kubla Khan is slain!
And ravaged lies his vast domain!"
And stood I there within my ghosted gown, enshrouded,
White and wild it billow'd 'round,
And fixed my gaze on starless skies—
That sunny dome! Those caves of ice!
Such wonders wrought by such divine device!
'Til barbarous men and battle cries
Devoured Kubla's Paradise.

The jagged jewelled walls of all his gypsum caves
   were streaming
Down to cut clear crystal falls in bloody waves,
   with turmoil teeming,
Where Alph, the sacred river, ran
Through caverns measureless to man.
And far away, a harsh and heavy, heaving cloud
Breathed silent Kubla's funeral shroud.
Mossy tendrils heavy hung
All overgrown, and dared encloak,
Too proudly, stately walls and towers
Whose awesome power they once bespoke.
The shadow of the pleasure-dome
That floated midway on the waves,
Amidst the mingled measure of the fountain and
   the caves,
Upon the ocean lingered still,
And glistened on a sunless sea,
Held fast within its surge and sway:
The vestige of a dead decree.

And still this place had all the seeming
Of the fairyland of all my dreaming;
This savage land of seven suns
Was Heavenly in all its gleaming:
A Paradise where angels dwell,
Though demon winds blew straight from Hell.

The damsel with a dulcimer,
The mighty fount, the floating hair,
Still drift beneath my flashing eyes,
And still I seek and see them there.
By night, I hold within my keeping
Visions of a sleeper sleeping, dreaming
Dreams of rare device:
Of savage waves and caves of ice,
And forge once more that dome in air
And drink the draught of Paradise.

Acknowledgments

I would like to thank the following people for their constant encouragement and for their faith in me and my work:

My parents, John and Peggy Roberts, my dear friends, Carmen and Colin Willcox, Professor Ursula Irwin and the faculty and students of Mount Hood Community College, Freddie Wiltshire, Marc Lastrajoli, George Harvey, John Richardson, Pia Richardson, Dr. David Reesor, Robert Smith, Jim and Melanie Roberts, Petusha Berthel, Michael Pendragon of Pendragonian Publications, Gayle Oleska, Agi Willcox, Angela Kessler, Hyacinthe L. Raven of Via Dolorosa Press and the entire staffs of *Romantics Quarterly, The Storyteller* and *Dreams of Decadence.*

Previous Publications

"How Sweet the Night" appears in *Penny Dreadful*, issue eleven; "Ophelia" and "Rondel" appear in *Songs of Innocence*, issue two; "It Is Too Late" appears in *The Storyteller*, April 2000; "On Parting" appears in *The Storyteller*, July 2000; "Allayne" and "Ophelia" appear in *Erased, Sigh, Sigh,* volume three, issue one; "How Sweet the Night," "It Is Too Late" and "Skin & Bones" appear in *Erased, Sigh, Sigh*, volume three, issue two; "Clayre" and "Christine" appear in *Romantics Quarterly,* issue one; "Kubla Khan" appears in *Romantics Quarterly,* issue two; "Rondel" scheduled to appear in *The Storyteller*, October 2000; "Mortiche," "Elfin Charms," "Chainmail Angel," "Ophelia" and "Alone" scheduled to appear in upcoming issues of *Dreams of Decadence.* "Allayne" and "Skin & Bones" scheduled to appear in *Penny Dreadful,* issue twelve. "Mortiche" and others scheduled to appear in upcoming issues of *Songs of Innocence.*

Other books available from CC Productions

At Home in Paradise   B105   **£6.95**

At Home in Paradise is the irresistibly intimate journal of a sensitive and impassioned observer of Nature. From the attic of her 16th Century farmhouse in the English Countryside, Carmen records her impressions of the most subtle movements of Nature that ripple through her daily existence at the pace of some distant childhood summer, quietly yet profoundly influencing her Inner Life. Reminiscent of Thoreau's Walden in its appreciation of the Natural World as a nurturing, guiding and powerful force, Carmen's journal also calmly celebrates the beauty and sanctuary available in the 'tiny pleasures' of everyday life.

Pocketful of Paradise   B109   **£6.95**

In her first prose journal "At Home In Paradise", Carmen introduced us to an enchanted world of natural beauty intimately capturing the essence of English country life with its rich variety of lively activity. Now, in "Pocketful of Paradise", its pocket-sized companion, the popular poet and journalist again invites us to journey along as she guides us through another radiant year of intriguing, and at times humorous, pastoral happenings. With wonder and enthusiasm, lending equal space to the commonplace and the unusual, Carmen observes and comments on Nature's grand displays and its subtle surprises. Through lyrical, beautifully-wrought images of silver moon-lit gardens and emerald 'oceans' sprinkled with buttercups, we are drawn into her magical realms, surrounded by a fascinating assembly of wildlife (particularly her beloved bevy of colourful wild birds) some just seasonal visitors, others who make Paradise Farm their perennial home.

SpellBound   B104   £6.95

Spellbound is a volume of magical, otherworldly beauty that will drench your soul with untamed yet holy insights into the shadowy, forbidden reaches of the human heart, revealing strange truths and extraordinary beauty. These poems, accented by lavish, inspiring artwork, are a wonderful introduction to the mystical revelations of Carmen's writings, viewing the world through the exquisitely melancholic haze of the lover's most rapturous dreams.

Luminarium
In Search of the DreamChild   B101   £6.95

Through dreamlike images and the enchantment of language, one enters a mystical labyrinth, a kingdom that unveils the timeless power of light and innocence. Our inner journeys, our impassioned pleas, the sacredness of love and the sublime intensity of spiritual longings; are all movingly captured in over 50 poems. Profusely illustrated with Classic and Pre-Raphaelite images.

Gothic Dream   B102   £6.95

Gothic Dream is an elegant and visionary glimpse of other realms. It is a bridge to a parallel dimension, a romantic world of inconsolable beauty and exquisite passions, wrapped in a web of lyrical sensuality. 120 pages of intriguing and enthralling poems, masterfully crafted and beautifully illustrated throughout with woodcuts and Pre-Raphaelite line drawings.

Sorrows of Fleeting Joy   B103   £6.95

With the eloquence and depth of the great Romantic poets, Carmen unveils a singularly graceful insight into the human spirit's intensely passionate quest for immortal, loving union. Often erotic and sensuous, always poignant and captivating, these poems lure the reader into a sustained and compelling glimpse of a magical world where the souls of lovers ride the wings of Eternity in their desire to experience love on the level of the Divine. You will discover yourself within its inspired pages.

Quest For the Beloved   B106   £6.95
       by Kevin N. Roberts

In this personal, philosophical approach to Carmen's Romantic and Metaphysical poetry, Professor Roberts takes an unprecedented look at the role of poetry as a tool for individual spiritual growth. The author reveals that, as a means of gaining a greater understanding of the human condition, the potential of Metaphysical poetry to unveil the nature of true romantic love, the loss of youthful innocence and the mysterious realm that awaits us all beyond death, is virtually without limit. At once authoritative, accessible and engaging, *Quest for the Beloved* will appeal not only to poetry lovers, but to anyone interested in following their bliss!

How To Order These Books:

Simply list your choices and send your name and address with
payment (Cheque, P.O. or Access/Visa number)
plus £1.95 total P&P to:

New World Music, The Barn, Becks Green, Beccles, Suffolk
NR34 8NB England

Tel: 01986 781 682 / Fax: 01986 781 645

Request a free colour Catalogue,
including recordings featuring Carmen's Poetry.